Break**fast**

For

Champions

50 High-Protein, High-Fiber
Recipes to Fuel Your Morning

By

Astrid Dwight

Table of Contents

Introduction...6

50 High-Protein, High-Fiber Recipes for Breakfast......................10

Protein-Packed Oatmeal..10

Veggie-Packed Scrambled Eggs.......................................11

Quinoa Breakfast Bowl 12

Greek Yogurt Parfait 13

Peanut Butter Banana Smoothie 13

Chia Seed Pudding..14

Spinach and Mushroom Breakfast Wrap 15

Blueberry Protein Pancakes 15

Avocado Toast with Poached Eggs 16

High-Protein Breakfast Burrito 17

Cottage Cheese and Fruit Bowl.......................................19

Nutty Banana Breakfast Burrito 19

Veggie Frittata 20

Apple Cinnamon Quinoa Bowl.......................................21

High-Fiber Chia Muffins 22

Tropical Protein Smoothie 22

Peanut Butter Banana Overnight Oats 23

Green Protein Smoothie Bowl 24

Mediterranean Egg Scramble...24

High-Fiber Banana Walnut Muffins...................................25

Berry-Almond Chia Smoothie 26

Sweet Potato and Black Bean Hash...................................27

Protein-Packed Banana Pancakes 27

High-Protein Berry Parfait...28

Blackberry Protein Smoothie 29

Fiber-Rich Breakfast Cookies 30

Pumpkin Protein Pancakes..30

Berry Quinoa Breakfast Bowl..31

Chia and Mixed Fruit Parfait 32

Protein-Packed Breakfast Burrito Bowl.............................32

Raspberry Almond Smoothie...33

Banana Nut Overnight Oats...34

High-Fiber Chocolate Zucchini Muffins.............................34

Mixed Berry Protein Crepes...35

High-Protein Chocolate Smoothie 36

Veggie and Cheese Omelette...38

Peanut Butter Banana Breakfast Quesadilla 38

Veggie-Packed Breakfast Burrito.......................................39

Protein-Packed Cottage Cheese Bowl 40

High-Fiber Apple Cinnamon Muffins...................................41

Chocolate Banana Protein Smoothie.................................41

Greek Yogurt and Berries Stuffed Crepes 42

Savory Breakfast Quinoa..43

High-Protein Berry Muffins..43

Tropical Chia Seed Pudding..44

High-Fiber Banana Walnut Bread.......................................46

Spinach and Feta Egg Muffins...46

High-Fiber Banana Nut Pancakes 47

Protein-Packed Breakfast Wrap 48

High-Protein Berry Crumble...49

Conclusion...50

Introduction

In the quiet corner of a busy town, where the first rays of dawn painted the sky with hues of gold and rose, a magical transformation unfolded each morning. The aroma of sizzling bacon, simmering oats, and fresh fruits danced through the air, leading me to a quaint, welcoming kitchen.

Nestled at the heart of this culinary haven was a collection of recipes like no other, captured within the pages of my creation. These pages whispered stories of vitality, energy, and the remarkable journey of the champions who indulged in these creations.

In these captivating tales, the amalgamation of high-protein and high-fiber ingredients took center stage. As I explored these recipes, I realized that the secret to my thriving morning ritual lay in the combination of protein and fiber. The protein, with its power to rebuild and fortify, stood as a pillar of strength. And the fiber, with its gentle yet assertive touch, ensured that my day started with a steady surge of energy that lasted long past the morning haze.

Amidst the vivid descriptions of fluffy protein-packed pancakes and hearty fiber-rich granolas, the unspoken benefits of this magical alliance shone bright. I found myself embodying a vitality that transcended the page, thanks to the protein's ability to build lean muscle and the fiber's gift of sustained fullness.

As the stories unraveled, I experienced improved digestion, controlled blood sugar levels, and the kind of mental clarity that only a nutrient-rich morning could offer. With every turn of the page, I embarked on a voyage of understanding, discovering how the harmonious blend of protein and fiber could set the tone for a day filled with achievement and vigor.

This collection of recipes was more than just a cookbook; it was a portal into a world where the power of a morning meal extended beyond the plate. It was a promise of nourishment, a celebration of the synergy between protein and fiber, and an invitation to partake in the everyday magic that transformed ordinary mornings into extraordinary beginnings.

50 High-Protein, High-Fiber Recipes for Breakfast

Dive into a world of vibrant mornings with these 50 high-protein, high-fiber breakfast recipes. From wholesome oatmeal creations to energizing smoothies, each recipe is a culinary journey that fuels your day with vitality and nourishment. Discover the perfect balance of flavors, textures, and nutrients to kickstart your mornings and set the tone for a champion's day ahead.

Protein-Packed Oatmeal

Ingredients:
- Rolled oats
- Almond milk
- Chia seeds
- Greek yogurt
- Mixed berries.

Preparation:
- Cook oats in almond milk
- Mix in chia seeds

- Top with Greek yogurt and berries.

Nutritional Value (approx. per serving):
- 300 calories
- 20g protein
- 10g fiber.

Veggie-Packed Scrambled Eggs

Ingredients:
- Eggs
- Spinach
- Bell peppers
- Onion
- Feta cheese.

Preparation:
- Scramble eggs, sauté vegetables
- Mix in feta cheese.

Nutritional Value (approx. per serving):
- 250 calories
- 18g protein

- 5g fiber.

Quinoa Breakfast Bowl

Ingredients:
- Cooked quinoa
- Black beans
- Avocado
- Salsa
- Cilantro.

Preparation:
- Mix quinoa and black beans
- Top with avocado, salsa, and cilantro.

Nutritional Value (approx. per serving):
- 350 calories
- 15g protein
- 12g fiber.

Greek Yogurt Parfait

Ingredients:
- Greek yogurt
- Mixed nuts

- Money
- Mixed berries.

Preparation:
- Layer Greek yogurt
- Nuts
- Honey
- Berries in a glass.

Nutritional Value (approx. per serving):
- 280 calories
- 15g protein
- 8g fiber.

Peanut Butter Banana Smoothie

Ingredients:
- Banana
- Peanut butter
- Spinach
- Almond milk
- Chia seeds.

Preparation:
- Blend all ingredients until smooth.

Nutritional Value (approx. per serving):

- 350 calories
- 12g protein
- 8g fiber

Chia Seed Pudding

Ingredients:

- Chia seeds
- Almond milk
- Vanilla extract
- Sliced almonds.

Preparation:

- Mix chia seeds, almond milk, and vanilla
- Refrigerate overnight
- Top with sliced almonds.

Nutritional Value (approx. per serving):

- 220 calories
- 8g protein
- 10g fiber

Spinach and Mushroom Breakfast Wrap

Ingredients:

- Whole wheat tortilla

- Scrambled eggs
- Sautéed spinach
- Mushrooms.

Preparation:
- Assemble scrambled eggs, sautéed veggies in the tortilla
- Wrap, and enjoy.

Nutritional Value (approx. per serving):
- 280 calories
- 18g protein
- 6g fiber

Blueberry Protein Pancakes

Ingredients:
- Whole wheat flour
- Protein powder
- Egg whites
- Blueberries.

Preparation:
- Mix ingredients
- Cook pancakes
- Top with fresh blueberries.

Nutritional Value (approx. per serving):

- 220 calories
- 20g protein
- 5g fiber

Avocado Toast with Poached Eggs

Ingredients:

- Whole grain toast
- Poached eggs
- Mashed avocado
- Red pepper flakes.

Preparation:

- Spread avocado on toast
- Top with poached eggs
- Sprinkle red pepper flakes.

Nutritional Value (approx. per serving):

- 280 calories
- 15g protein
- 7g fiber

High-Protein Breakfast Burrito

Ingredients:
- Whole wheat tortilla
- Scrambled eggs
- Black beans
- Shredded cheese

Preparation:
- Fill tortilla with eggs, black beans, cheese
- Wrap, and warm.

Nutritional Value (approx. per serving):
- 330 calories
- 20g protein
- 8g fiber

Cottage Cheese and Fruit Bowl

Ingredients:
- Cottage cheese
- Mixed fruit (berries, peaches, etc.)
- Honey.

Preparation:
- Top cottage cheese with mixed fruit and drizzle with honey.

Nutritional Value (approx. per serving):
- 220 calories
- 15g protein
- 5g fiber

Nutty Banana Breakfast Burrito

Ingredients:
- Whole wheat tortilla
- Almond butter
- Ssliced bananas
- Chopped nuts.

Preparation:

- Spread almond butter on tortilla
- Add sliced bananas
- Sprinkle nuts
- Wrap.

Nutritional Value (approx. per serving):

- 280 calories
- 10g protein
- 6g fiber

Veggie Frittata

Ingredients:

- Eggs, bell peppers
- Tomatoes
- Onion
- Spinach

Preparation:

- Whisk eggs
- Mix in veggies
- Bake until set

Nutritional Value (approx. per serving):
- 200 calories
- 15g protein
- 4g fiber

Apple Cinnamon Quinoa Bowl

Ingredients:
- Cooked quinoa
- Chopped apples
- Cinnamon
- Chopped nuts.

Preparation:
- Mix quinoa, apples, and cinnamon
- Top with nuts.

Nutritional Value (approx. per serving):
- 240 calories
- 10g protein
- 6g fiber

High-Fiber Chia Muffins

Ingredients:
- Whole wheat flour
- Chia seeds
- Greek yogurt
- Honey.

Preparation:
- Mix ingredients
- Bake muffins until golden.

Nutritional Value (approx. per muffin):
- 180 calories
- 7g protein
- 5g fiber

Tropical Protein Smoothie

Ingredients:
- Pineapple
- Mango
- Greek yogurt
- Protein powder
- Almond milk.

Preparation:

- Blend all ingredients until smooth.

Nutritional Value (approx. per serving):

- 300 calories
- 20g protein
- 6g fiber

Peanut Butter Banana Overnight Oats

Ingredients:

- Rolled oats
- Almond milk
- Peanut butter
- Sliced bananas.

Preparation:

- Mix oats, almond milk, and peanut butter
- Refrigerate overnight
- Top with banana slices

Nutritional Value (approx. per serving):

- 350 calories
- 15g protein
- 8g fiber

Green Protein Smoothie Bowl

Ingredients:
- Spinach
- Banana
- Protein powder
- Almond milk
- Chia seeds

Preparation:
- Blend ingredients until smooth
- Pour into a bowl
- Top with chia seeds

Nutritional Value (approx. per serving):
- 280 calories
- 18g protein
- 10g fiber

Mediterranean Egg Scramble

Ingredients:
- Eggs
- Cherry tomatoes
- Feta cheese
- Black olives
- Fresh basil

Preparation:
- Scramble eggs
- Add tomatoes, olives, and feta
- Garnish with basil.

Nutritional Value (approx. per serving):
- 250 calories
- 15g protein
- 4g fiber

High-Fiber Banana Walnut Muffins

Ingredients:
- Whole wheat flour
- Mashed bananas
- Chopped walnuts
- Flaxseeds.

Preparation:
- Mix ingredients
- Bake muffins until cooked through

Nutritional Value (approx. per muffin):

- 180 calories
- 6g protein
- 7g fiber

Berry-Almond Chia Smoothie

Ingredients:
- Mixed berries
- Almond milk
- Chia seeds
- Almond butter

Preparation:
- Blend ingredients until smooth

Nutritional Value (approx. per serving):
- 230 calories
- 8g protein
- 10g fiber

Sweet Potato and Black Bean Hash

Ingredients:
- Sweet potatoes
- Black beans

- Red onion
- Bell peppers
- Cumin

Preparation:
- Sauté ingredients until cooked
- Season with cumin.

Nutritional Value (approx. per serving):
- 300 calories
- 12g protein
- 8g fiber

Protein-Packed Banana Pancakes

Ingredients:
- Ripe bananas
- Protein powder
- Egg whites
- Cinnamon

Preparation:
- Blend ingredients
- Cook pancakes
- Sprinkle with cinnamon

Nutritional Value (approx. per serving):
- 250 calories
- 18g protein
- 5g fiber

High-Protein Berry Parfait

Ingredients:
- Greek yogurt
- Mixed berries
- Almonds
- Honey

Preparation:
- Layer yogurt, berries, almonds, and drizzle with honey.

Nutritional Value (approx. per serving):
- 260 calories
- 18g protein
- 6g fiber

Blackberry Protein Smoothie

Ingredients:

- Blackberries
- Protein powder
- Almond milk
- Greek yogurt

Preparation:

- Blend all ingredients until smooth.

Nutritional Value (approx. per serving):

- 280 calories
- 20g protein
- 7g fiber

Fiber-Rich Breakfast Cookies

Ingredients:

- Rolled oats
- Mashed bananas
- Raisins
- Ground flaxseeds

Preparation:

- Mix ingredients
- Form into cookies
- Bake until golden

Nutritional Value (approx. per cookie):

- 150 calories
- 5g protein
- 4g fiber

Pumpkin Protein Pancakes

Ingredients:

- Pumpkin puree
- Protein powder
- Egg whites
- Pumpkin spice

Preparation:

- Mix ingredients
- Cook pancakes
- Sprinkle with pumpkin spice

Nutritional Value (approx. per serving):

- 220 calories

- 20g protein
- 6g fiber

Berry Quinoa Breakfast Bowl

Ingredients:
- Cooked quinoa
- Mixed berries
- Chopped almonds
- Honey

Preparation:
- Combine quinoa, berries, almonds, and drizzle with honey.

Nutritional Value (approx. per serving):
- 290 calories
- 12g protein
- 8g fiber

Chia and Mixed Fruit Parfait

Ingredients:
- Chia seeds
- Almond milk
- Mixed fruit (kiwi, mango, etc.)

Preparation:
- Mix chia seeds with almond milk
- Layer with mixed fruit.

Nutritional Value (approx. per serving):
- 260 calories
- 8g protein
- 10g fiber

Protein-Packed Breakfast Burrito Bowl

Ingredients:
- Scrambled eggs
- Black beans
- Quinoa
- Salsa
- Avocado

Preparation:
- Assemble scrambled eggs, beans, quinoa, salsa, and avocado.

Nutritional Value (approx. per serving):
- 350 calories
- 20g protein
- 10g fiber

Raspberry Almond Smoothie

Ingredients:
- Raspberries
- Almond milk
- Protein powder
- Almond butter

Preparation:
- Blend all ingredients until smooth.

Nutritional Value (approx. per serving):
- 240 calories
- 18g protein
- 8g fiber

Banana Nut Overnight Oats

Ingredients:
- Rolled oats
- Almond milk
- Chopped nuts
- Sliced bananas

Preparation:

- Combine oats, almond milk, nuts
- Refrigerate overnight
- Add bananas

Nutritional Value (approx. per serving):
- 320 calories
- 10g protein
- 8g fiber

High-Fiber Chocolate Zucchini Muffins

Ingredients:
- Whole wheat flour
- Grated zucchini
- Cocoa powder
- Chopped walnuts.

Preparation:
- Mix ingredients
- Bake muffins until cooked through

Nutritional Value (approx. per muffin):
- 180 calories
- 6g protein
- 6g fiber

Mixed Berry Protein Crepes

Ingredients:
- Crepe batter
- Mixed berries
- Greek yogurt
- Honey

Preparation:
- Make crepes
- Fill with yogurt and berries
- Drizzle with honey.

Nutritional Value (approx. per serving):
- 280 calories
- 12g protein
- 5g fiber

High-Protein Chocolate Smoothie

Ingredients:
- Chocolate protein powder
- Almond milk
- Banana

- Chia seeds.

Preparation:
- Blend all ingredients until smooth

Nutritional Value (approx. per serving):
- 290 calories
- 22g protein
- 7g fiber

Veggie and Cheese Omelette

Ingredients:
- Eggs
- Bell peppers
- Onion
- Spinach
- Feta cheese

Preparation:
- Make omelette
- Fill with veggies and cheese

Nutritional Value (approx. per serving):
- 220 calories
- 16g protein
- 4g fiber

Peanut Butter Banana Breakfast Quesadilla

Ingredients:
- Whole wheat tortilla
- Peanut butter
- Sliced banana
- Honey

Preparation:
- Spread peanut butter on tortilla
- Add banana slices
- Drizzle with honey
- Fold and warm.

Nutritional Value (approx. per serving):
- 300 calories
- 10g protein
- 6g fiber

Veggie-Packed Breakfast Burrito

Ingredients:
- Scrambled eggs
- Black beans
- Bell peppers
- Onions
- Salsa

Preparation:
- Assemble eggs, beans, veggies, salsa in a tortilla
- Wrap, and warm

Nutritional Value (approx. per serving):
- 320 calories
- 15g protein
- 8g fiber

Protein-Packed Cottage Cheese Bowl

Ingredients:
- Cottage cheese
- Sliced almonds
- Mixed berries
- Honey

Preparation:
- Mix cottage cheese with almonds, berries
- Drizzle with honey.

Nutritional Value (approx. per serving):
- 280 calories
- 20g protein
- 5g fiber

High-Fiber Apple Cinnamon Muffins

Ingredients:
- Whole wheat flour

- Grated apple
- Cinnamon
- Chopped walnuts

Preparation:
- Mix ingredients
- Bake muffins until cooked through.

Nutritional Value (approx. per muffin):
- 170 calories
- 5g protein
- 7g fiber

Chocolate Banana Protein Smoothie

Ingredients:
- Chocolate protein powder
- Almond milk
- Banana
- Oats.

Preparation:
- Blend all ingredients until smooth.

Nutritional Value (approx. per serving):
- 320 calories
- 25g protein

- 6g fiber

Greek Yogurt and Berries Stuffed Crepes

Ingredients:
- Crepe batter
- Greek yogurt
- Mixed berries
- Honey

Preparation:
- Make crepes
- Fill with yogurt and berries
- Drizzle with honey.

Nutritional Value (approx. per serving):
- 250 calories
- 12g protein
- 6g fiber

Savory Breakfast Quinoa

Ingredients:
- Cooked quinoa
- Scrambled eggs
- Baby spinach
- Cherry tomatoes

Preparation:

- Combine quinoa, eggs, spinach, tomatoes
- Sauté until heated

Nutritional Value (approx. per serving):

- 280 calories
- 15g protein
- 8g fiber

High-Protein Berry Muffins

Ingredients:

- Protein powder
- Oats
- Mixed berries
- Egg whites

Preparation:

- Mix ingredients
- Bake muffins until golden.

Nutritional Value (approx. per muffin):

- 180 calories

- 15g protein
- 4g fiber

Tropical Chia Seed Pudding

Ingredients:
- Chia seeds
- Coconut milk
- Diced pineapple
- Shredded coconut

Preparation:
- Mix chia seeds with coconut milk
- Refrigerate
- Top with pineapple and coconut

Nutritional Value (approx. per serving):
- 250 calories
- 8g protein
- 10g fiber

High-Fiber Banana Walnut Bread

Ingredients:
- Whole wheat flour
- Mashed bananas
- Chopped walnuts
- Flaxseeds

Preparation:
- Mix ingredients
- Bake as a loaf until cooked through

Nutritional Value (approx. per slice):
- 180 calories
- 5g protein
- 6g fiber

Spinach and Feta Egg Muffins

Ingredients:
- Eggs
- Baby spinach
- Crumbled feta cheese
- Diced tomatoes

Preparation:
- Whisk eggs

- Mix in spinach, feta, and tomatoes
- Bake in muffin cups.

Nutritional Value (approx. per muffin):
- 150 calories
- 10g protein,
- 4g fiber

High-Fiber Banana Nut Pancakes

Ingredients:
- Whole wheat flour
- Mashed bananas
- Chopped nuts
- Ground flaxseeds

Preparation:
- Mix ingredients
- Cook pancakes
- Serve with sliced bananas

Nutritional Value (approx. per serving):
- 260 calories

- 8g protein
- 7g fiber

Protein-Packed Breakfast Wrap

Ingredients:
- Whole wheat tortilla
- Scrambled eggs
- Lean turkey
- Spinach

Preparation:
- Assemble eggs, turkey, spinach in tortilla
- Wrap, and warm.

Nutritional Value (approx. per serving):
- 300 calories
- 20g protein
- 5g fiber

High-Protein Berry Crumble

Ingredients:
- Mixed berries

- Oats
- Protein powder
- Almond butter

Preparation:
- Mix berries, oats, protein powder
- Top with almond butter
- Bake until golden

Nutritional Value (approx. per serving):
- 280 calories
- 15g protein
- 8g fiber

Congratulations! You now have a diverse collection of 50 high-protein, high-fiber breakfast recipes that will energize and nourish your mornings. Remember to adjust ingredients and portion sizes based on your dietary preferences and needs. Enjoy these delicious creations as you embark on each day feeling invigorated and ready to tackle anything that comes your way!

Conclusion

In the heart of the busy town, where each morning began with the promise of something extraordinary, there stood a cozy kitchen that held the stories of champions. A collection of recipes had woven a tapestry of flavors and nourishment, igniting vitality and determination in those who dared to embrace its offerings.

As the sun rose over the horizon, casting its gentle glow on the town, the aroma of sizzling creations invited all to partake in this magical culinary journey. With each dish lovingly crafted, the champions found themselves propelled into a realm of well-being, where high-protein and high-fiber breakfasts became the cornerstone of their days.

The vibrant tales of energy-infused oatmeal, bold and protein-packed smoothies, and savory burritos brimming with wholesome ingredients had carved a path toward stronger bodies, sharper minds, and unstoppable spirits. From students striving for success to athletes pushing their limits, the pages of the cookbook bore witness to their transformation into champions of their own lives.

As the seasons changed and time marched forward, the legacy of these recipes endured. Morning after morning, the legacy carried on—a legacy that proclaimed that every day was an opportunity to rise, nourish, and conquer. And within each dish, a message resonated: The power to champion your day begins with the choices you make in the morning.

So, dear reader, with this collection of 50 high-protein, high-fiber breakfast recipes, you now hold the key to crafting your own tale of vitality. Let the magic of each ingredient infuse your mornings with energy, health, and the unwavering belief that you can conquer anything that comes your way. Embrace the flavors, savor the nourishment, and remember:

"Fuel Your Morning, Conquer Your Day!"

Made in United States
North Haven, CT
03 November 2023

43563932R00028